Discover & Learn

Mayan Civilisation

This book is perfect for pupils studying the Mayan civilisation in KS2 History (ages 7-11).

It's jam-packed with facts, sources and questions covering the history and achievements of the Maya — perfect for exploring and understanding the whole topic.

Published by CGP

Contributor: Sarah Elsdon

Editors: Catherine Heygate, Katya Parkes

ISBN: 978 1 78294 969 5

With thanks to Janet Berkeley and Alex Fairer for the proofreading.

With thanks to Jan Greenway for the copyright research.

Printed by Elanders Ltd, Newcastle upon Tyne

Clipart from Corel®

Text, design, layout and original illustrations © Coordination Group Publications Ltd. (CGP) 2018

All rights reserved.

Photocopying more than one section of this book is not permitted, even if you have a CLA licence.
Extra copies are available from CGP with next day delivery • 0800 1712 712 • www.cgpbooks.co.uk

Contents

Meet the Maya

In the jungles and hills of Central America, lie the ruins of a society that has fascinated historians for decades — the Maya. By around AD 900, the Maya were an <u>astonishingly advanced</u> society with their own ways of doing everything from farming to maths.

Early days

When the Maya arrived in Central America's jungles around <u>12 000 years ago</u>, they were hunter-gatherers. They didn't live in one place, but <u>travelled around</u> to find food. Over time, they learnt how to <u>farm</u>, and this allowed them to stay in one place and begin building <u>permanent settlements</u>. Between about 2000 BC and AD 250, Mayan settlements grew. Some developed into <u>large cities</u> like El Mirador.

Timeline

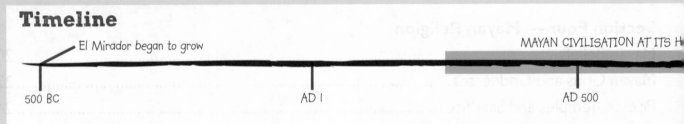

El Mirador began to grow

MAYAN CIVILISATION AT ITS H

500 BC   AD 1   AD 500

At the peak of the pyramid

Between AD 250 and AD 900, Mayan civilisation was at its height. The Maya built <u>huge cities</u> throughout Central America, many of which had <u>massive populations</u>. For example, historians think that Caracol was home to more than 100 000 people by AD 900.

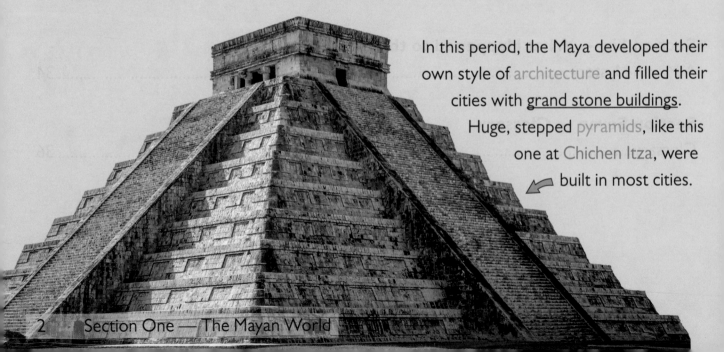

In this period, the Maya developed their own style of architecture and filled their cities with <u>grand stone buildings</u>. Huge, stepped pyramids, like this one at Chichen Itza, were built in most cities.

A mysterious disappearance...

Around AD 900, some huge cities in the south of the Mayan territory, like Tikal and Copán, were suddenly <u>abandoned</u>. Historians aren't sure why this happened, although lots of weird and wonderful theories have been put forward (page 34).

Can you think of any reasons why a city might be abandoned?

Although the Maya left some cities at this point, those in the north continued to <u>grow</u> for hundreds of years. In AD 1500, Mayan society was still thriving, but it was about to change forever...

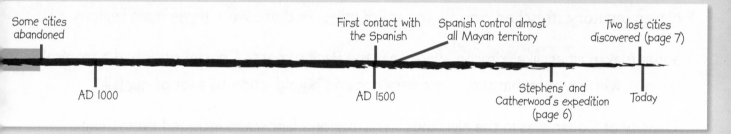

Some cities abandoned

AD 1000

First contact with the Spanish

AD 1500

Spanish control almost all Mayan territory

Stephens' and Catherwood's expedition (page 6)

Two lost cities discovered (page 7)

Today

The fall of the Maya

In the early 1500s, <u>Spanish invaders</u> arrived in Mayan territory and began <u>fighting</u> the Maya to take control of their land. The Spanish had to defeat most Mayan cities separately, but by the 1540s they had taken control of <u>almost all</u> Mayan territory.

Geniuses in the jungle

The Maya were a very advanced bunch who built a successful society. They were experts in architecture and maths, and invented their own calendars, sports, writing system, farming methods and religion. Pretty impressive, right? Turn over to find out more...

Riches in the Rainforest

Mayan territory was in Central America. It was spread across several modern-day countries — Mexico, Belize, Guatemala, Honduras and El Salvador.

> Have you heard of any of these countries before? What do you know about them?

The Maya built more than <u>60 cities</u>, most of which are found in modern-day Mexico and Guatemala. Some of the most <u>important</u> cities are shown on the map.

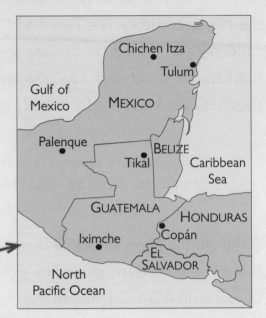

Jungles, volcanoes and coasts

Mayan territory stretched over <u>thousands of miles</u> — there were <u>three</u> main regions.

Some Mayan cities, like Iximche, were near the <u>Pacific coast</u>. Coastal cities had a <u>tropical climate</u>, which meant that they were very <u>hot</u> and <u>humid</u>, and had a lot of <u>rainfall</u>.

The city of Copán was in the <u>highlands</u>. This region's landscape included everything from snowy mountain ranges and <u>volcanoes</u> to lush <u>forests</u>.

The picture below shows the city of Palenque in the <u>lowlands</u>. This region was home to a huge range of <u>wildlife</u> and hundreds of species of trees. Some trees could grow to be 70 metres tall!

People of the land

Conditions could be <u>tough</u> in some parts of the Mayan territory, but the Maya were very skilled at <u>adapting</u> to their surroundings. They found clever ways to use the resources around them in their daily lives.

The Maya built many <u>grand cities</u> entirely out of materials that could be found in the local area. Mayan builders used <u>wood</u> from the rainforests and limestone that they dug out of the earth (page 12) with tools made from <u>stone</u>.

Flint is a hard, sharp stone which the Maya used to make tools and weapons. These are examples of flint objects made by the Maya.

Can you think of any other societies that used flint?

Mayan farmers often struggled to find <u>farmland</u>, but they invented <u>new farming techniques</u> (page 16) that made it easier for them to grow crops.

What are the key features of the landscape where you live? How have people adapted to the landscape? Have they altered it in any way?

Jungle gems

The picture on the right shows a bird called a quetzal. Resources such as quetzal feathers, cacao beans and precious stones like jade were only found in certain parts of Mayan territory. Because they were hard to find, they were very <u>valuable</u> to the Maya. Wealthy Maya would use them to show off how <u>rich</u> and <u>powerful</u> they were.

How the landscape made the Maya...

Mayan territory covered around 324 000km² — that's much bigger than Britain! Their land was varied and could be difficult to survive in. However, the Maya found ways to adapt, and their inventive solutions enabled them to build a thriving and successful society.

Hidden Cities

Ruins of Mayan settlements can be found across much of Central America. By exploring these ruins, archaeologists can learn a lot about what life was like in ancient Mayan societies.

Deep in the jungle...

For hundreds of years, ruined Mayan cities lay <u>abandoned</u> in the forests of Central America. Few people from outside the region even knew that they were there.

Despite being over a thousand years old, the ruins of most Mayan cities are in <u>good condition</u>. Archaeologists excavate them to uncover <u>buildings</u> and all sorts of other <u>Mayan objects</u>. The things they find give us lots of information about how the Maya lived and what their culture was like.

In 1839, two explorers, <u>John Lloyd Stephens</u> and <u>Frederick Catherwood</u>, set out on a daring expedition to Central America. They trekked through the jungle, making records of the <u>abandoned Mayan cities</u> that they found. They were so fascinated by the sites, that Stephens even bought the ruins at Copán for 50 dollars! The picture below of a temple at Tulum was drawn by Catherwood.

Why do you think that Mayan ruins are often in such good condition?.

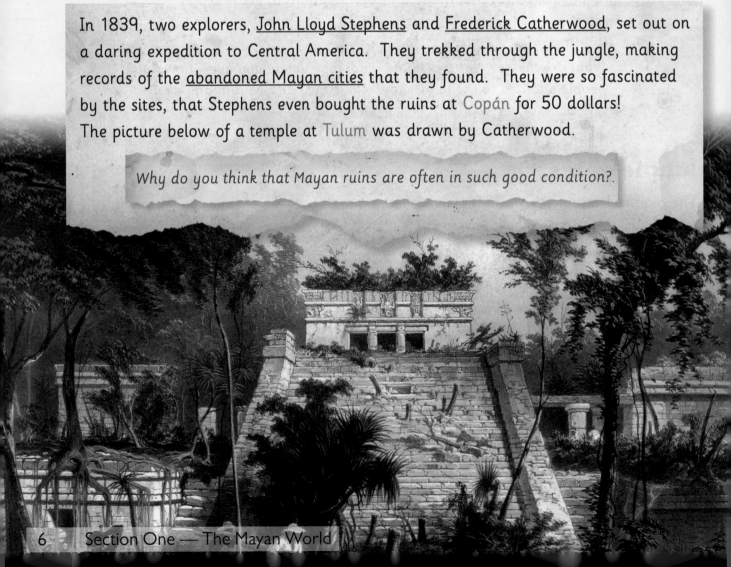

Seeing the sites

One of the <u>largest</u> and most <u>impressive</u> Mayan sites that archaeologists have discovered so far is the city of Tikal in modern-day Guatemala.

Here, archaeologists found towering <u>temples</u>, huge <u>palaces</u>, defensive city walls and detailed stone <u>carvings</u>.

Cracking finds

Archaeologists have found more than just buildings. They often unearth hard-wearing objects like <u>pottery</u> and statues. Items such as <u>storage jars</u> and <u>cooking pots</u> give us a better idea of what the Maya ate and how they prepared their food. <u>Statues</u> of gods can help us to understand more about Mayan <u>religion</u>.

Raided ruins

Over time, a lot of Mayan objects have been <u>lost</u> or <u>destroyed</u>. Some items, like textiles, have simply rotted away. Other objects were burned or smashed by <u>Spanish invaders</u> in the 1500s (page 35). <u>Thieves</u> have also stolen a lot of art and pottery from Mayan ruins to sell.

The best is yet to come?

There's still a lot we don't know about the Maya — there are probably even some abandoned cities that <u>haven't been discovered</u> yet. As recently as <u>2014</u>, archaeologists found two new cities in Mexico called Tamchen and Lagunita. Instead of trekking through the jungle like Stephens and Catherwood, they spotted them on <u>photographs</u> taken from the air.

The mysterious Maya...

Even though Mayan cities lay abandoned for hundreds of years, they're still brimming with information. From temples to cooking pots, every discovery teaches us something new.

Inside a City State

Mayan territory was split into city states, most of which were <u>independent</u> of one another. Each state was made up of a <u>city</u> and the <u>farmland</u> and <u>villages</u> around it. The city was home to the state's ruling family, other powerful people and the most important buildings.

Friends or enemies?

Not only were most Mayan city states <u>independent</u>, they were also <u>far apart</u>. Despite this, city states had <u>contact</u> with each other. Merchants often travelled between them to <u>trade</u> (pages 18-19).

However, city states didn't always get along. If rulers <u>disagreed</u>, then violence or even <u>war</u> could break out. The city states of Calakmul and Tikal were fierce enemies and fought for decades. The wall painting on the left shows a battle between Mayan warriors.

The heart of the city state

In the centre of many Mayan cities there was a large, <u>open square</u> where markets were held (pages 18-19). Grand temple-pyramids (pages 24-25) towered over many Mayan cities and there were also <u>ball courts</u> (page 26) and <u>platforms</u> used for religious rituals.

The ruling family often lived in single-storey <u>palaces</u> in the city centre, and wealthy Maya also had houses in the city. Poorer people lived in <u>simple</u> homes outside the city.

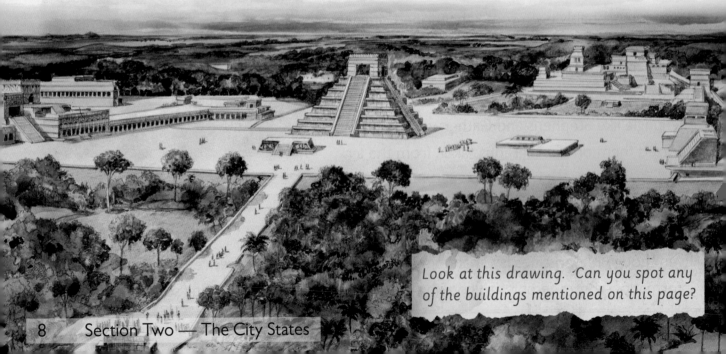

Look at this drawing. Can you spot any of the buildings mentioned on this page?

Chichen Itza

Chichen Itza is in modern-day Mexico. It was one of the largest Mayan city states and also a major <u>trade centre</u> — people from all across Central America would travel there to buy and sell goods.

A lot of the art and buildings found at Chichen Itza <u>aren't</u> in the <u>traditional</u> Mayan style. This may be because different styles were brought to the city state by traders and visitors from <u>outside</u> Mayan territory.

<u>El Castillo</u> is a huge pyramid at the centre of Chichen Itza. Some people believe that the Maya designed this pyramid so that if you clap your hands in front of it, the echo sounds like the call of the <u>quetzal</u> — a sacred bird in Mayan culture (page 5).

El Mirador

El Mirador, which is in modern-day Guatemala, was at its most powerful around 2000 years ago. At that time, El Mirador was a massive city state which was home to <u>tens of thousands</u> of people. The city is famous for its enormous buildings, especially the La Danta pyramid, which is one of the <u>largest</u> pyramids in the world.

Caracol

Caracol is in modern-day Belize. At its peak, between AD 550 and AD 900, it was much bigger than the largest city in Belize today. The pyramid at Caracol is called <u>Caana</u>, which means 'sky place'. At 42 metres tall, it's still the <u>highest</u> man-made structure in Belize. Caracol was known for its success in battle — its warriors won many wars against neighbouring city states.

Mayan cities – they're in a pretty good state...

The Mayan city states never formed a single nation, but they had a lot in common. They shared a similar language and religion, and many used similar styles of art and architecture.

Mayan Rulers

Each city state had its own ruler, and these rulers were very powerful people.
They were in charge of making all the most important <u>decisions</u> within their city state.

The chosen one

The Maya believed that rulers were given their power by the gods.
They thought rulers could contact the gods through bloodletting rituals.

This carving shows a <u>bloodletting ritual</u>. A Mayan queen is pulling a <u>spiky rope</u> through her <u>tongue</u>, then collecting the blood as an <u>offering</u> for the gods. The Maya believed that rulers had to keep up a good relationship with the gods to ensure that their city state would be successful.

Do you think the Maya might have blamed their rulers when bad things happened in their city state? Why?

Royal responsibilities

Rulers' sons were taught how to rule from <u>birth</u>. It is thought that one young prince took part in his first bloodletting ritual at just <u>five years old</u>.

Rulers were expected to <u>defeat</u> enemies and <u>protect</u> their people. They had to be fierce and successful <u>warriors</u> who could control the <u>army</u> in times of war. At a young age, they could be sent into battle to prove themselves.

Other royal duties included <u>hosting</u> visitors from other city states, managing <u>trade</u> routes and sharing out <u>water</u>.

K'inich Yax K'uk' Mo'

Historians think that <u>K'inich Yax K'uk' Mo'</u> was originally a warrior from Tikal. In AD 426, he conquered the city state of Copán and became its ruler. He built a new city there, which grew to be a <u>rich</u> and <u>successful</u> trade centre. His family ruled Copán for around 400 years.

Pakal the Great

<u>Pakal the Great</u> (AD 603-AD 683) was only twelve when he became ruler of Palenque. He ruled the city state for nearly <u>70 years</u>. Under him, Palenque became grand and powerful. Pakal was given a spectacular burial when he died — his <u>funeral mask</u> was made entirely from jade.

Would you have wanted to be a Mayan ruler? Why?

Girls rule!

Mayan rulers were usually men, but city states sometimes had <u>female</u> rulers. <u>Lady Yohl Ik'nal</u> ruled over Palenque for 20 years between AD 583 and AD 604 with all the power that a male ruler would have had.

Between AD 672 and AD 692, <u>Lady K'abel</u> and her husband ruled El Perú-Waka'. Lady K'abel was known as '<u>supreme warrior</u>' — historians think this means that she was <u>more powerful</u> than her husband.

A royal life of luxury?

Mayan rulers may have had power and wealth, but their lives weren't always particularly glamorous. They had a lot of different duties and responsibilities, some of which could be dangerous and painful — like going to war or taking part in bloodletting rituals.

Mayan Buildings

Using only <u>simple</u> tools and materials, the Maya built enormous cities. Their construction techniques were so successful that many of their buildings are still standing today.

Back to the stone age...

The buildings in most Mayan cities were made of limestone. This stone is <u>common</u> in Central America, so it's likely that city states had their own quarries where workers would cut huge blocks of limestone out of the earth.

> *What do you think working in a Mayan quarry would have been like?*

Limestone was an ideal building material — it's soft enough to dig up, but it quickly hardens after that. Even though limestone was easy to find in Mayan territory, it was an <u>expensive</u> material. It was only used to build <u>public buildings</u> and the homes of <u>rich</u> Maya.

Heavy lifting

The Maya didn't have <u>vehicles with wheels</u> or strong <u>animals</u> like horses to help them move stone from the quarry to the city, so they had to do it themselves. We think that they loaded blocks of stone onto <u>log rollers</u>, which they then <u>pulled</u> through the jungle. To construct buildings, the blocks were stuck together with a sort of <u>cement</u>.

> *Most Mayan buildings were just one storey high. Why do you think this might have been?*

Exclusive addresses

Wealthy Maya built spectacular homes in the city centre to show how <u>rich</u> and <u>powerful</u> they were. Houses were built using <u>limestone</u> and were decorated with <u>carvings</u> and <u>pillars</u>. Wealthy Maya didn't just choose limestone to show off — it also <u>protected</u> their houses against bad weather, fire and enemy attacks.

This is the Governor's Palace at Uxmal. The homes of wealthy Maya were often built on <u>high platforms</u> to make them seem <u>more important</u> than other buildings.

Home sweet home

Poorer Maya lived in <u>simple</u> houses outside of the city centre. They built their homes from materials they found in the <u>jungle</u> — they used <u>wood</u> for the frame, <u>palm leaves</u> for the roof and <u>vines</u> to tie everything together. This picture shows what a poorer person's house might have looked like.

Most huts only had <u>one room</u>. One half of the room was probably used for living in during the day and the other half for sleeping. Families often built a <u>group of huts</u> and lived next door to each other.

We think that the Maya may have built separate huts for different activities, such as <u>cooking</u> and <u>storage</u>.

Why do you think archaeologists know more about the houses of rich Maya than poorer Maya?

Ahead of their time...

It's very impressive that the Maya were able to construct and decorate their buildings with such limited technology. Using only tools made from stone and wood — and of course lots of manpower — the Maya built huge cities that have lasted for thousands of years.

Fashion and Beauty

Appearance meant a lot to the Maya. Fashion could be used to show how important you were, so the Maya went to extreme lengths to achieve the perfect look...

High-class fashion

The Maya used clothes to show how rich and powerful they were. While ordinary people wore plain, <u>simple</u> clothes, wealthy people's clothes were brightly <u>coloured</u> and <u>decorated</u>.

Men often wore a <u>cape</u> called a <u>pati</u>. Rich Maya might own a pati made from jaguar skins and decorated with brightly coloured feathers and embroidery.

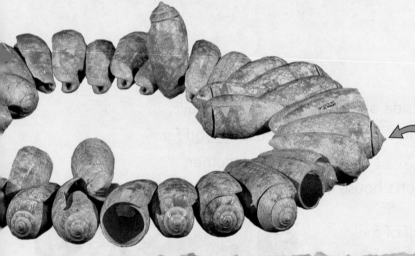

People also used <u>jewellery</u> to show their wealth. Rich people had necklaces made of shells, jade, gold and even jaguar teeth. Poor people wore simpler jewellery made of bone and wood.

Do people today still use what they wear to show how important they are? What would you wear if you were dressing to impress?

Turning heads

Rulers and noblemen wore huge colourful <u>headdresses</u>. They decorated them with jade, shells, jaguar skins and carvings of gods and animals. <u>Feathers</u> were used too — the Maya even bred certain birds especially to use their feathers in headdresses. These feathers could be up to a metre long.

Extreme makeovers

The Maya did some <u>extreme</u> things to <u>change</u> their bodies and make them look a certain way.

The god of maize was often shown with a <u>pointed</u>, <u>flattened</u> face. The Maya thought that this look was very attractive and tried to copy it. Parents gently pressed their baby's head between two boards — over time, this made its forehead <u>slope up</u> and <u>backwards</u>.

<u>Crossed eyes</u> were another popular feature. Parents would hang tiny <u>balls</u> in front of their child's face so that their eyes would become permanently crossed!

No pain, no gain...

<u>Tattoos</u> were popular among the Maya. They would <u>paint</u> a design onto their skin, then cut along the lines of the design. The <u>scar</u> would form a coloured tattoo.

The Mayan king in this statue has his <u>ears pierced</u> with huge discs of stone. The Maya achieved this look by piercing their ears, then forcing pieces of jade or other stones into the piercing.

The Maya thought that having <u>sharp teeth</u> was beautiful, so they would file their teeth to a point. They might then <u>drill holes</u> into their teeth and decorate them with jade.

How do Mayan ideas of beauty compare to those we have today? Do we still do any of the same things to our bodies?

Fashion victims

It seems that some Mayan trends were pretty painful, but fashion and beauty were important parts of Mayan culture. The Maya used fashion to show off their power and wealth, to honour the gods and simply to make sure they looked their best.

Food and Farming

Mayan farmers had to deal with <u>rainforests</u>, <u>swamps</u> and <u>steep hillsides</u>. They didn't have animals to help them and their only tools were made from stone and wood. Despite these challenges, Mayan farmers were extremely <u>successful</u>.

Jungle farming

One common Mayan farming technique was called <u>slash and burn</u>. Farmers would <u>chop down</u> trees then set <u>fire</u> to the area. The <u>ash</u> from the fire added <u>nutrients</u> to the soil, which made it easier for crops to grow.

<u>Terrace farming</u> was used to grow crops on steep hills. The Maya would cut <u>ledges</u> into the side of a hill, then build <u>walls</u> to support them. This would stop soil <u>slipping down</u> the slope and make <u>space</u> to plant crops.

Mayan menu

The Maya grew a lot of maize (also called corn). Maize was so important to the Maya that it was even <u>worshipped</u> as a god (page 23). The Maya grew other crops too, such as beans, squash, sweet potatoes, avocados, tomatoes, papaya and chilli peppers. They also <u>fished</u> in the rivers and <u>hunted</u> for deer, turtles and a wild pig called a <u>peccary</u>.

Do you eat any of the foods that the Maya ate?

Ready... steady... cook!

The Mayan diet was <u>varied</u> and what people ate depended on <u>where</u> their city state was. Historians think that a kind of maize <u>porridge</u> called <u>atole</u> was a popular dish. Most other meals would probably have contained lots of vegetables as well as some meat or fish. <u>Tortillas</u> (a flatbread made from maize) were served with every meal.

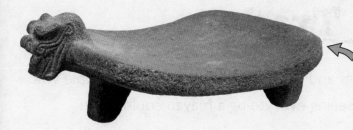

A grinding stone, or <u>metate</u>, was an important tool in every Mayan kitchen. <u>Soaked maize</u> was put onto the metate, then crushed until it formed a <u>dough</u> that was made into <u>tortillas</u>.

Chocoholics

<u>Chocolate</u> is made from the beans of the cacao tree. Chocolate as we know it today was only invented in the 19th century, but the Maya had their own way of serving cacao. They would grind cacao beans into a paste and make it into a drink called <u>xocoatl</u> which they flavoured with <u>spices</u> and <u>chilli</u>.

Would you prefer to drink xocoatl or modern hot chocolate? Why?

This drawing shows two Maya watching a bubbling pot of xocoatl. Cacao beans were very <u>valuable</u>, so it is thought that xocoatl was mostly drunk by <u>rich</u> people.

Because cacao beans were so precious, the Maya sometimes used them as money to pay for things at the market.

So... money does grow on trees?

Mayan city states had very large populations. This meant that Mayan farmers had to work hard to grow enough crops to feed everyone. To do this, they used some inventive farming methods — some of which are still used by farmers all over the world today.

Mayan Trade

Trade was a key part of Mayan culture. Traders and merchants were powerful people who travelled across Central America and beyond selling everything a Mayan could want.

Linking up the city states

Each Mayan city state was good at producing some things but lacked others. For example, city states in the highlands produced lots of jade and obsidian, but they didn't have many cacao beans, which were mainly found in the lowlands. A trade network developed between city states, so that goods from all over the Mayan region could be bought and sold.

The city states didn't just trade with each other. Mayan merchants also took their goods to other societies in ⬅ Central America — the Aztecs traded copper in return for Mayan cacao beans, feathers and jaguar skins.

The Maya may even have been involved in trade with places much further away, such as South America.

Off to market

The picture below shows the ruins of El Mercado in Chichen Itza. Historians think that it may have been the city's marketplace. Mayan markets would have been pretty rowdy places — many of them even employed people to settle arguments between shoppers!

Not exactly travelling light...

Mayan merchants didn't have vehicles with wheels or animals to carry their goods, so they hired groups of porters to do it instead. These people had to walk many miles between city states, carrying huge loads on their backs.

What do you think life as a porter might have been like?

Some merchants also used large, wooden <u>canoes</u> to transport their goods by river or sea. Even though the Maya were expert sailors, travelling by water could be dangerous. <u>Hurricanes</u> and tropical storms were common, so the seas were sometimes very rough.

Set out your stall

All sorts of goods could be found at a Mayan market. Local farmers would bring food, such as maize, meat, fruit, vegetables and honey. Some merchants brought <u>everyday</u> items, like salt, tools and textiles. Others traded <u>luxury</u> goods, such as jade, jewellery and even gold items like this one.

<u>Raw materials</u>, including obsidian, flint and wood, were traded at markets. <u>Craftspeople</u> traded their work too — embroidery, baskets, pottery and paper were all on offer.

Most trade was done by <u>bartering</u> — one item would be <u>swapped</u> for another. Luxury items could be paid for with valuable goods, such as cacao beans and jade.

How do Mayan markets compare to the places where you go shopping? What are the differences? Can you think of any similarities?

Hustle and bustle

People from all levels of society could be found at a Mayan market — from ordinary people buying food and clothes to rich Maya buying luxury goods to show off their wealth.

Mayan Beliefs

Mayan religious beliefs are still a bit of a <u>mystery</u> to us today. This is because Mayan religion was very <u>complicated</u> and people's beliefs <u>varied</u> from region to region.

A Mayan history book

The <u>Popol Vuh</u> is a book of Mayan myths and <u>history</u> which contains lots of useful information about Mayan religion. However, it was written in <u>the 1500s</u>, long after the time in Mayan history that it describes, and it <u>only</u> contains the views of <u>one group</u> of Maya.

Do you think we can trust the information in the Popol Vuh?

The creation story

The Maya believed that the gods created humans. According to the Popol Vuh, the gods first tried making humans out of <u>mud</u> and then out of <u>wood</u>. However, they weren't happy with either of these versions, so they <u>destroyed</u> them.

Next, they tried making humans out of maize. The gods were <u>pleased</u> with these humans, but they were worried that they were <u>too wise</u>.

Instead of destroying these humans, the gods put a <u>mist</u> over their eyes to make them <u>less wise</u>. The Maya believed that this was why humans weren't as clever as gods.

What does this story tell you about why maize was so important to the Maya?

The layers of life

The Maya thought that the universe was made up of lots of different <u>layers</u>. As well as the <u>visible earth</u> where <u>people</u> lived, they believed that there were <u>invisible layers</u> above and below the earth where the <u>gods</u> and <u>spirits</u> of the dead lived. They thought that the Tree of Life linked all the layers together. The carving on the left is thought to show the Tree of Life.

The Maya believed that the earth was flat — some even thought that the earth's surface was the back of a huge turtle! Another Mayan belief was that the sky was held up by four strong gods called Bacabs.

Life after death?

The Maya believed in <u>life after death</u>. They thought that some people went straight to <u>paradise</u>, where there was no work or pain, and plenty of food and drink to enjoy.

It was thought that rulers, priests, warriors, women who died in childbirth and people who were sacrificed or who killed themselves went to paradise.

Others went to a cold, dark <u>underworld</u> called Xibalba which was ruled over by the <u>god of death</u>. The Maya believed that <u>caves</u> could be entrances to Xibalba, so they used them as places to <u>bury</u> their dead.

The way of the world...

It can be tricky to make sense of Mayan religious beliefs, because different groups of Maya had different ideas about heaven and hell, life and death, and everything in between.

Mayan Gods and Goddesses

The Maya believed in many different gods and goddesses, who were linked to every part of their lives — from weather and war to crops and rainbows.

Changing identities...

Archaeologists find Mayan gods a bit confusing and it's easy to see why. Sometimes the <u>same</u> god was known by <u>different names</u> in different regions or at different times in Mayan history.

Ideas about the gods and what they looked like <u>varied</u> a lot too. At different times, the same god might be shown as young or old, male or female, human or animal and even good or evil. Despite this, archaeologists have been able to work out who some of the <u>most important</u> gods were by studying Mayan pottery, paintings and writings.

Itzamna

Itzamna was the <u>creator god</u> and was often shown as <u>king</u> of the gods. The Maya often drew him as an old man with no teeth and a long nose, but sometimes he's shown as a kind of lizard called an <u>iguana</u>! Itzamna was the god of medicine too, and he's even supposed to have invented writing and books. He was also the <u>first</u> Mayan priest.

Look at what Itzamna is wearing in this picture. How can you tell that he was very important?

Hun Hunahpu

Hun Hunahpu was the god of maize. Mayan myths said that he died each year at harvest time and was born again when the new growing season began. He was very important to the Maya because he brought the seasons and the maize they needed to survive.

Hun Hunahpu was a kind god, who was often shown as a young, handsome man. The Maya adored him so much that they tried to look like him (page 15), and Mayan rulers dressed as him for festivals.

Chaak

Chaak was the god of rain. He was shown as half-human, half-reptile, with scales, fangs and a curling snout. He often carried an axe or a lightning bolt.

Farmers worshipped Chaak so that he would bring the rains they needed for their crops, but they also feared him — he could bring awful storms and floods.

K'inich Ahau

K'inich Ahau was the sun god. He had T-shaped teeth and crossed eyes, which the Maya saw as beautiful. Kings used his name because they believed they were similar to him.

The Maya believed that during the day, K'inich Ahau provided the warmth and light that crops needed to grow. By night, they thought he became a jaguar and visited Xibalba.

Would you have been scared of any of the Mayan gods? Why?

A god for everything...

Mayan gods and goddesses were believed to be extremely powerful. They could affect every part of Mayan life, and if they were unhappy they could cause all sorts of disasters, from famines to floods. Turn over to find out how the Maya kept their gods happy...

Priests, Temples and Sacrifices

Mayan priests were thought to receive <u>messages</u> from the gods, which they passed on to the Maya. This made priests very important people — only the ruler was more powerful.

Priestly powers

Priests were highly <u>educated</u>. They could read and write, and were experts in maths and astronomy. This carving shows a priest.

One of a priest's most important jobs was carrying out <u>ceremonies</u> to please the gods. These ceremonies usually started with feasting, dancing and music, then <u>offerings</u> were made to the gods. The offerings might have been things like incense and food, but sometimes they included blood or even grisly <u>human sacrifices</u>.

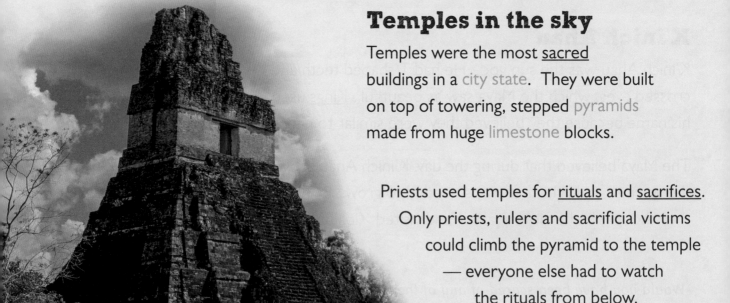

Temples in the sky

Temples were the most <u>sacred</u> buildings in a city state. They were built on top of towering, stepped pyramids made from huge limestone blocks.

Priests used temples for <u>rituals</u> and <u>sacrifices</u>. Only priests, rulers and sacrificial victims could climb the pyramid to the temple — everyone else had to watch the rituals from below.

Why do you think only certain people were allowed to climb up to the temple?

The temples themselves were small, but the pyramids they stood on could be enormous. The pyramids at Tikal are extremely tall — one temple there stands at 70 metres! Pyramids and temples were painted with bold colours and decorated with beautiful carvings.

Gruesome rituals

The Maya believed that they had to give offerings to the gods to keep them happy. The most extreme way of providing an offering was through human sacrifice — usually of slaves or prisoners of war. Methods of sacrifice included shooting the victim with a bow and arrow, beheading them or removing their heart while it was still beating.

Human sacrifices were quite rare — they were held to mark special occasions, like a new king coming to the throne or a new temple being built. They might have happened more often during droughts and famines, as the Maya tried to make the gods happy again.

Royal bloodletting rituals (page 10) were another way the Maya tried to please the gods. Rulers cut their ears or tongue and offered the blood to the gods. The carving on the left shows a Mayan queen communicating with a god during a bloodletting ritual.

The Maya thought that it was an honour to take part in rituals like these. Would you have felt the same?

It's all about give and take

From building massive pyramids to suffering pain and even death, the Maya went to extremes to make sure the gods were on their side. They believed that in return for these efforts, the gods would bless their city state with wealth and success.

The Game of Death

Most Mayan city centres had ball courts where the Maya played a game called <u>Pok-A-Tok</u>. The game could be played for <u>fun</u>, but sometimes it was used as a deadly <u>religious ritual</u>.

A sacred game

The <u>Hero Twins</u> were sons of the maize god. The Maya believed that they had once annoyed the gods of the underworld by playing Pok-A-Tok too loudly. As a punishment, the gods summoned the twins to Xibalba and gave them challenges — they <u>outsmarted</u> the gods every time.

The twins wanted to <u>escape</u>, so they showed the gods that they could bring people back to life. This impressed the gods so much that they asked to be killed and reborn. The twins killed them but didn't bring them back to life — then they seized their chance to escape from Xibalba.

Why do you think Pok-A-Tok meant so much to the Maya?

Court in the middle

The picture below shows the ruins of a Pok-A-Tok court. Courts were shaped like an 'I' and usually had two long, <u>sloping walls</u>. There were <u>stone rings</u> high up on both of the sloping walls. Courts varied in size, but the <u>largest</u> one ever found is a huge 166 metres long.

Play by the rules

No-one really knows what the rules of Pok-A-Tok were. We think that the game was played by two teams who had to pass a rubber ball using only their knees, hips, elbows and wrists.

It is thought that players scored points by knocking the ball into the other team's area or making a shot the other team couldn't return. If a player managed to get the ball through one of the stone rings, their team instantly won. A version of Pok-A-Tok is still played in Central America today — the picture on the right shows a modern player.

Can you think of any similarities between Pok-A-Tok and modern-day sports?

A must-win game?

Pok-A-Tok wasn't just played for fun. Prisoners of war were sometimes forced to play against a city state's rulers. If the prisoners lost (and they always did), they would be killed.

The game was also played for religious reasons. The Maya thought that ball courts were gateways to the underworld, and they sometimes played Pok-A-Tok as a religious ritual with players acting out the story of the Hero Twins.

Historians aren't sure what happened when these ritual games ended. Some say that the winning team was rewarded by being sacrificed — this would mean they'd go straight to heaven. Others say that the losing team was killed.

Pok-A-Tok wasn't all fun and games...

...it was quite literally a game of life and death! Pok-A-Tok matches were held in the city centre and were big, popular events — much like sports matches today. People from all levels of society, including the city state's rulers, would sometimes take part in the games.

Writing and Maths

One of the great Mayan inventions was their writing system. The way they recorded words and numbers was so complex that historians still don't fully understand it today.

The Mayan language

The Maya used hundreds of <u>symbols</u> called hieroglyphs to write things down. Some hieroglyphs stood for a certain word or phrase. These hieroglyphs often looked like the thing they represented. For example, this is the hieroglyph for the word 'jaguar'.

Other hieroglyphs represented specific syllables. By putting lots of hieroglyphs together, the Maya recorded important events and wrote down stories and myths.

This diagram shows how to read a Mayan text. The Maya read from left to right — just as we do. However, they tackled their texts two columns at a time. After reading across two hieroglyphs, they would move to the row below and start again.

Do you think Mayan hieroglyphs would have been easy or difficult to read? Why?

Cracking the code

Mayan writing is pretty <u>tricky</u> to decode. Some hieroglyphs had several meanings and lots of them <u>changed</u> over time. To make matters worse, the Maya often <u>mixed</u> hieroglyphs together or put one inside another — very confusing!

Historians only started to understand Mayan writing properly from the 1950s. They now think that they recognise about <u>800 hieroglyphs</u>, but there are still some that they don't understand.

Reading is power

The Maya thought that writing was a <u>sacred</u> gift from the gods, so only certain people called scribes were taught to read and write. These <u>skills</u> made scribes important people.

Rulers employed scribes to write down what happened in their city states. This picture shows a scribe at work.

Write it down

The Maya wrote about everything from politics to plants. <u>Buildings</u>, monuments, <u>pottery</u> and <u>ornaments</u> could all be decorated with texts.

The Maya also wrote lots of books, called codices. These were written on paper made out of <u>bark</u> and decorated with hieroglyphs and pictures. Sadly, Spanish invaders <u>destroyed</u> almost all these books in the 1500s — we think that <u>only three survive</u> today.

Easy as dot, dot dot, dot dot dot

The Maya invented a new <u>number system</u>, as well as a way to record numbers. They worked out difficult maths using only three symbols — a <u>shell</u> which meant zero, a <u>dot</u> which meant one and a <u>dash</u> which meant five.

Mayan maths was based around the number 20. This might be because people worked out sums by counting on their <u>fingers</u> and <u>toes</u>.

The writing's on the wall

Spanish invaders may have burned thousands of Mayan books, but they didn't wipe out Mayan writing completely. Thanks to all the writing on Mayan buildings and monuments, historians can still decode Mayan hieroglyphs and use them to learn about the Maya.

Stargazers

The Maya were experts at astronomy. They kept track of the sun, moon, stars and planets, and used this information to make calendars.

Written in the stars

The Maya had two separate calendars, the Haab and the Tzolkin, which worked at the same time. Each day had two different dates — one from each calendar.

The Haab

The Haab lasted for 365 days. It was split up into 18 months that were each 20 days long. The last five days of the calendar were a separate month, which was thought to be very unlucky. The Maya avoided doing anything during that month because they believed they were at risk of danger and death. In the diagram, the days of the Haab are shown in the green boxes.

The Tzolkin ⟶

Priests used the Tzolkin to decide the dates of important events like battles and religious rituals. They even used it to predict the future. The Maya believed that the god who represented your birthday in the Tzolkin had an influence over your entire life.

The Tzolkin lasted for 260 days. Each day had a name, which was made by combining one of 20 day names with a number between one and thirteen. In the diagram, the day names are in the yellow ring and the numbers one to thirteen are in the red ring.

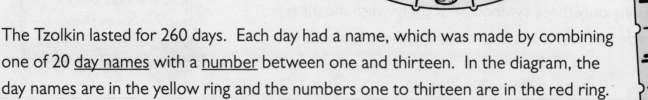

Are there any similarities between the Mayan calendars and our calendar?.

Expert astronomers

Mayan priests were <u>skilled</u> astronomers. By studying the sky, they could accurately predict solstices, eclipses and equinoxes.

The Maya believed that the sun, moon, planets and stars were all <u>gods</u> who could <u>affect</u> their lives. Priests watched the movements of these objects in the skies carefully to <u>plan</u> when important events should take place and to make <u>predictions</u> about what might happen on earth. The Maya recorded some of these predictions in their codices.

This drawing shows a prediction of a great flood.

Stellar buildings

The Maya chose the <u>locations</u> of important buildings like temples and pyramids carefully so that they lined up with <u>astronomical events</u>. Pakal the Great's (page 11) tomb at Palenque is lined up with the sun, so that at sunset on the <u>winter solstice</u>, the light appears to go down the stairs to his tomb.

This is an observatory at Chichen Itza called <u>El Caracol</u>. Its position is lined up with the path of the planet <u>Venus</u>. The Maya watched Venus because they thought that the planet was linked with <u>war</u>. Generals only went to war when Venus was in a certain position in the sky.

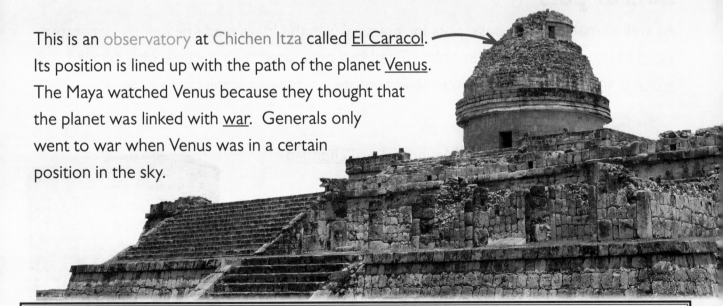

Heads in the clouds

Mayan priests kept a close eye on the skies. The movements of the stars and planets told them when to hold <u>rituals</u>, let farmers know when to plant their crops and were even thought to help predict the future! Reading the sky was a powerful skill...

Mayan Art

The Maya were talented craftspeople. From murals to carvings, they produced a huge variety of artworks, as well as simpler objects for everyday tasks like cooking.

Set in stone

<u>Carvings</u> were produced in every Mayan city state. The walls of buildings and the steps of pyramids were decorated with carved hieroglyphs and pictures. The Maya also decorated columns of limestone called <u>stelae</u> with carvings of their rulers. The picture on the right shows one of the stelae at Copán.

Some artists made smaller carvings from valuable materials like jade. Because jade is very <u>hard</u>, it was difficult to carve. Artists had to be highly <u>skilled</u> to produce carvings like this one of the sun god, K'inich Ahau.

Lots of pots

As well as making plain, basic pots for practical use, the Maya made beautifully <u>decorated</u> <u>vases</u> to use in religious ceremonies. The Maya decorated their pottery with detailed <u>writings</u> and <u>images</u> — sometimes telling stories or showing scenes from Mayan myths.

The style and decoration of Mayan pottery <u>changed</u> over time. This is really <u>useful</u> to historians — it means that just by looking at a piece of pottery, they can often work out <u>when</u> it was made.

Look at this vase. It shows some Mayan warriors in battle. What do you think historians could learn about the Maya and Mayan soldiers by studying this vase?

The bigger picture

The walls in important buildings like palaces and tombs were often painted with scenes from Mayan life and myths.

This painting is based on the mural that covers the walls of a building at Bonampak. The huge mural records battle scenes, royal events and religious rituals. It tells us simpler things about the Maya too, such as what they looked like and the clothes they wore.

Looming large

Mayan textiles were usually produced by women, who were experts in spinning, weaving and dyeing cloth. The fabrics they made were very colourful and were decorated with lots of embroidery.

This statue shows a woman weaving on a back-strap loom. This kind of loom had strings stretched between two sticks. A cord joined the sticks and wrapped around the weaver, so she could control the loom just by leaning back.

Modern Maya still use back-strap looms to produce colourful textiles. Each colour in modern Mayan cloth represents part of their history. For example, yellow stands for maize and green represents the quetzal and royalty.

A picture is worth a thousand words

With their carvings, murals and sculptures, the Maya filled their cities with art. Art was clearly very important to the Maya, and it plays a big role in studying them today. It helps give us a better idea of Mayan society and lets us see what their lives were really like.

A Mayan Mystery

Around AD 900, lots of city states in the south of the Mayan region were suddenly abandoned — and no-one really knows why. Further north, other city states continued to grow for several centuries until the arrival of Spanish invaders in the 16th century.

Disappearing act

Historians aren't sure why the Maya left city states like Copán, Tikal and Palenque — everything from erupting volcanoes and earthquakes to alien abduction has been suggested. However, it's likely that the Maya left because the city states could no longer support them.

By AD 900, some city states had huge populations, but they didn't have enough food or land for so many people. Food shortages were probably made worse by Mayan farming methods (page 16), which may have damaged their land. These problems probably led to conflict as communities began to fight over things like food and good farmland.

This wall painting shows Mayan warriors in battle. It was painted at Bonampak at the end of the 8th century. Soon afterwards, the city was abandoned.

Here come the Spanish...

Although the <u>southern</u> Mayan city states had long since been <u>abandoned</u>, city states in the <u>north</u>, such as Tulum, continued to <u>thrive</u> until the 16th century.

However, in 1502 the Spanish arrived in Mayan territory. They fought with the Maya for decades, and by the 1540s they had taken control of <u>most</u> of the Mayan region.

> *How do you think the Maya felt about the Spanish invasion?*

The Spanish claimed the best land and made the Maya work for them as <u>slaves</u>. They also forced the Maya to give up their religion and become <u>Christians</u>. The invaders <u>burned</u> thousands of Mayan books in an effort to stamp out the Mayan religion.

The Spanish brought European <u>diseases</u> with them that the Maya had never experienced before. These diseases <u>killed millions</u> of Maya.

A happy ending?

Today, there are about six million Maya still living in the same areas of Central America as their ancestors. Many of them have kept ancient Mayan <u>culture</u> and <u>traditions</u> alive.

Some Maya still speak the same <u>languages</u> and use the same <u>calendar</u> as their ancient ancestors. Farmers still plant maize, sometimes using ancient <u>methods</u>, and lots of traditional <u>crafts</u> like weaving are still practised. This photo shows a modern Mayan woman making cloth in the traditional way. The Mayan legacy looks set to live on...

Surviving against the odds

Famine, war, invasion, disease — the Maya have been through it all. Although parts of Mayan culture were destroyed by the Spanish invasion in the 16th century, many Mayan communities have managed to keep their identity and traditions alive and well.

Glossary

ancestor	A family member from long ago who someone is <u>descended</u> from.
archaeologist	A person who studies <u>history</u> by <u>digging up objects</u> and using them to find out more about the <u>past</u>.
architecture	The process of <u>designing</u> and <u>constructing</u> buildings.
astronomy	The study of <u>space</u>, the <u>objects</u> in space and the <u>universe</u>.
Aztecs	A <u>society</u> that lived to the <u>west</u> of the Maya in <u>Mexico</u>. The Aztecs were at their height between the 14th century and the 16th century.
bloodletting ritual	A <u>ritual</u> where the <u>ruler</u> of a city state <u>offered</u> their <u>blood</u> to the gods.
cacao	A <u>tree</u> whose bean-like <u>seeds</u> are used to make <u>chocolate</u>.
city state	An <u>independent state</u> made up of a <u>city</u> and the <u>farmland</u> and <u>villages</u> around it.
climate	The <u>weather conditions</u> in a certain <u>area</u>.
codex	An illustrated <u>book</u> made by the Maya. The plural of codex is <u>codices</u>.
eclipse	When one <u>object</u> in space <u>blocks</u> us from seeing another <u>object</u> in space. A <u>solar eclipse</u> is when the moon passes between the sun and the Earth.
equinox	When <u>day</u> and <u>night</u> are of <u>equal length</u>. There are two equinoxes every year.
excavate	Carefully <u>digging</u> in an area to find buried <u>remains</u> or ruins.
flint	A <u>hard</u>, <u>shiny</u> rock. When it's hit with something it <u>splits</u> into <u>sharp pieces</u>, so it can be used to make simple <u>tools</u> and <u>weapons</u>.
hieroglyph	A <u>picture</u> or <u>symbol</u> that represents a <u>word</u>, <u>phrase</u> or <u>sound</u>.
hunter-gatherer	A person who gets food by <u>collecting wild plants</u> and <u>hunting animals</u> instead of farming. They don't stay in one place, but <u>roam</u> around to find food.
incense	A substance that is burnt to give off a <u>sweet smell</u>.
jade	A <u>hard</u> stone that is usually <u>green</u>. The Maya often used jade to make <u>jewellery</u>.

jaguar	A big <u>cat</u> with a <u>yellow-brown</u> coat with black <u>spots</u>. Found in Central America. Jaguar skins were very <u>valuable</u> to the Maya.
limestone	A <u>rock</u> that is soft enough to dig out of the earth, but then quickly hardens. Limestone is often used for <u>building</u>.
loom	A <u>machine</u> used for <u>weaving threads</u> together to make <u>cloth</u>.
maize	A <u>grain</u> that is common in Central America.
merchant	A person who <u>buys</u> and <u>sells</u> goods.
mural	A <u>picture</u> painted directly onto a <u>wall</u>.
myth	A <u>traditional</u> story used by ancient societies to <u>explain</u> the world around them. Myths often involve <u>gods</u> and the <u>supernatural</u>.
observatory	A <u>specially designed</u> building where you can <u>study</u> the <u>stars</u> and <u>skies</u>.
obsidian	A <u>hard</u>, <u>black</u> rock. When it breaks, it has very <u>sharp</u> edges so it was often used as a <u>cutting</u> tool.
porter	A person whose job it is to <u>carry</u> goods or supplies.
priest	A <u>religious</u> leader. Mayan priests carried out <u>rituals</u> and studied the <u>stars</u>.
pyramid	A very <u>tall</u> building with <u>sloped</u> sides. The Maya built their temples on top of <u>stepped</u> pyramids.
quetzal	A <u>colourful bird</u> which can be found in Central America. The Maya considered it to be <u>sacred</u>.
scribe	A person who <u>copies</u> out documents or <u>writes down</u> the words of others.
solstice	There are <u>two</u> solstices every year. The <u>summer solstice</u> is the day with the <u>most</u> hours of sunlight. The <u>winter solstice</u> is the day with the <u>fewest</u>.
syllable	A <u>sound</u> within a word, usually made up of at least one <u>vowel</u> and sometimes also the <u>consonants</u> around it.
textiles	Pieces of <u>cloth</u> or woven material.
Xibalba	The name of the Mayan <u>underworld</u>. The Maya believed that some people went here when they <u>died</u>.

Picture Acknowledgements

Cover photo: © Peter Jackson / Look and Learn

Section One — The Mayan World

p3 (Copán sculpture) Dennis Cox / Alamy Stock Photo. p3 (Spanish invaders) Hernando Cortes (Cortez - 1485-1547) Spanish conquistador attacking natives in Mexico / Universal History Archive/UIG / Bridgeman Images. p4 (Palenque) Konstantin Kalishko / Alamy Stock Photo. p5 (flint objects) Sabena Jane Blackbird / Alamy Stock Photo. p6 (explorers) © Angus McBride / Look and Learn. p6 (Catherwood sketch) Granger Historical Picture Archive / Alamy Stock Photo. p7 (pottery) William Scott / Alamy Stock Photo. p7 (aerial ruins) Charles Wollertz / Alamy Stock Photo.

Section Two — The City States

p8 (wall painting) Granger Historical Picture Archive / Alamy Stock Photo. p8 (Chichen Itza drawing) The Chichen Itza complex, drawing, Mexico, Mayan civilization, 5th century BC-15th century AD / De Agostini Picture Library / Bridgeman Images. p9 (El Castillo) NATUREWORLD / Alamy Stock Photo. p10 (bloodletting) Science History Images / Alamy Stock Photo. p10 (wall painting) travelstock.ca / Alamy Stock Photo. p11 (K'inich Yax K'uk' Mo') © The Trustees of the British Museum. p11 (jade funeral mask) age fotostock / Alamy Stock Photo.

Section Three — Daily Life

p12 (Mayan quarry) Mayans remove bedrock to create a defensive wall at Punta de Chimino, 1993 (colour litho), Schlecht, Richard (b.1936) / National Geographic Creative / Bridgeman Images. p12 (transporting statue) © Peter Jackson/Look and Learn. p13 (house) beatrice preve / Alamy Stock Photo. p14 (vase painting) Heritage Image Partnership Ltd / Alamy Stock Photo. p14 (shell necklace) Necklace, from Topoxte, Peten, Guatemala, Late Classic Period (shell), Mayan / Museo Nacional de Arqueologia y Etnologia, Guatemala City / Jean-Pierre Courau / Bridgeman Images. p14 (headdresses) travelstock.ca / Alamy Stock Photo. p15 (god of maize) Stefano Ravera / Alamy Stock Photo. p16 (terraces) Al Argueta / Alamy Stock Photo. p17 (grinding stone) Grinding stone, Honduras, c.600-900 (basalt), Mayan / Collection of the Lowe Art Museum, University of Miami / Gift of Sylvia Coppersmith in memory of Dora Coppersmith / Bridgeman Images. p17 (xocoatl) The History Collection / Alamy Stock Photo. p18 (merchants) A bustling marketplace in the Aztec capital of Tenochtitlan, 1987 (colour litho), Hall, H. Tom (1932-2010) / National Geographic Creative / Bridgeman Images. p18 (ruins of El Mercado) imageBROKER / Alamy Stock Photo. p19 (porters) Historia General de las Cosas de Nueva Espana (General History of the Things of New Spain); written by trilingual Nahuatl, Spanish and Latin Aztec students of Sahagun;. p19 (golden disc) Golden disc from Los Limones, Ayutla, Guatemala, Post-Classic period (gold) / Jean-Pierre Courau / Bridgeman Images. p19 (pottery whistle) Panther Media GmbH / Alamy Stock Photo.

Section Four — Mayan Religion

p20 (Popol Vuh) Art Collection 3 / Alamy Stock Photo. p20 (creation story) Granger Historical Picture Archive / Alamy Stock Photo. p21 (Tree of Life carving) Stela 5 and associated Altar 36 at Izapa, late Pre-Classic Period (600 BC-100 AD) (stone) / Izapa, Chiapas, Mexico / Jean-Pierre Courau / Bridgeman Images. p21 (skull) World History Archive / Alamy Stock Photo. p22 (Mayan gods and goddesses) Chronicle / Alamy Stock Photo. p22 (Itzamna) The History Collection / Alamy Stock Photo. p23 (Hun Hunahpu) Granger Historical Picture Archive / Alamy Stock Photo. p23 (Chaak) Classic Image / Alamy Stock Photo. p23 (K'inich Ahau) Peter Horree / Alamy Stock Photo. p24 (priest) Granger Historical Picture Archive / Alamy Stock Photo. p25 (pyramids at Tikal) Hemis / Alamy Stock Photo. p25 (bloodletting) Peter Horree / Alamy Stock Photo. p26 (hero twins) Peter Horree / Alamy Stock Photo. p26 (Pok-A-Tok court) View of the ball game court and main plaza, Late Classic period (600-900 AD) (photo) / Copan, Honduras, Central America / Jean-Pierre Courau / Bridgeman Images. p27 (Pok-A-Tok player) Chico Sanchez / Alamy Stock Photo.

Section Five — Mayan Culture

p28 (jaguar hieroglyph) © Goran tek-en Licensed for re-use under the Creative Commons Attribution-ShareAlike 4.0 International (CC BY-SA 4.0). p28 (codex) age fotostock / Alamy Stock Photo. p29 (scribe) National Geographic Creative / Alamy Stock Photo. p29 (codex) The Print Collector / Alamy Stock Photo. p31 (flood prophecy) Peter Hermes Furian / Alamy Stock Photo. p32 (jade carving) World History Archive / Alamy Stock Photo. p32 (vase) Heritage Image Partnership Ltd / Alamy Stock Photo. p33 (Bonampak mural) Dennis Cox / Alamy Stock Photo. p33 (woman weaving) Figurine of a woman weaving / Werner Forman Archive / Bridgeman Images.

Section Six — What Happened to the Maya?

p34 (Bonampak painting) age fotostock / Alamy Stock Photo. p35 (Spanish invaders) Granger Historical Picture Archive / Alamy Stock Photo.